STEPHEN CURRY
My Secret To Success

Hello!

My name is Stephen Curry!

I'm a basketball player
who is an MVP!

But life for me wasn't always easy

Success is not an accident

And this is my story...

My secret to success....

I grew up wanting to be
like my father.
He was a great basketball
player!

But I was so small,
and my father was so tall.
Would I ever become
as great as him?

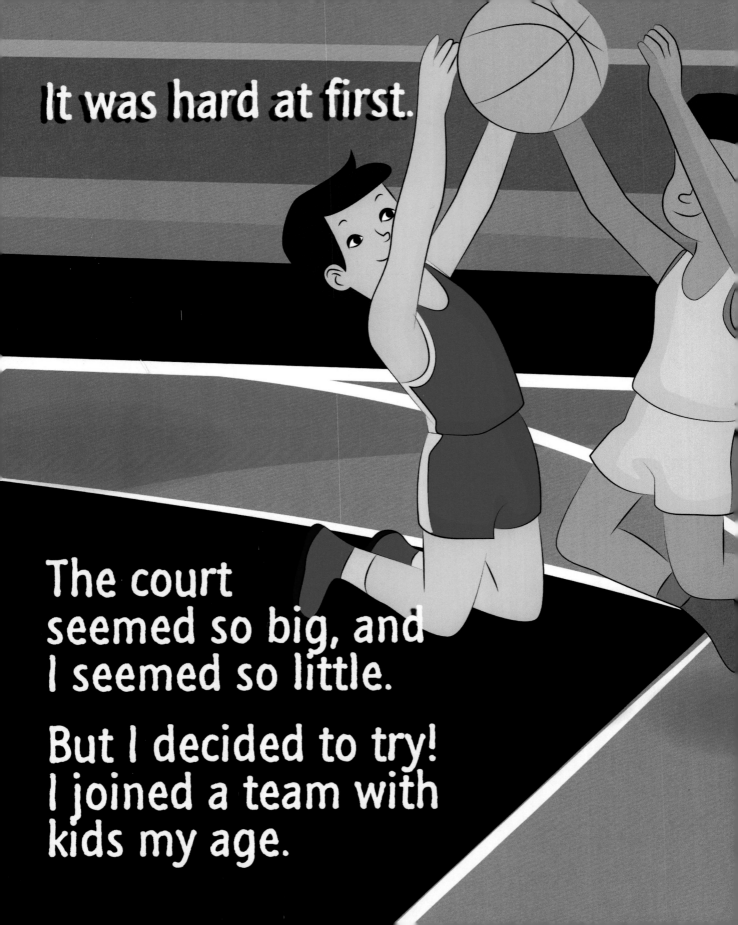

It was hard at first.

The court seemed so big, and I seemed so little.

But I decided to try! I joined a team with kids my age.

To my surprise, I had
my father's talent.
I'd dribble the ball and
throw it, the ball going into
the court with a swoosh!

All the other kids watched in surprise. I led the teams, and we won many games.

Sometimes, it wasn't that easy.

I'm not perfect.

I would drop the ball when my team needed it the most.

I'd throw the ball and
it would miss the goal
from a mile away.
I'd miss free throws.
I'd fall down.

The only difference was that I got back up.

I realized you can't be a star without falling a few times.

When people told me
I should quit, I kept
doing it.

When I thought I
wasn't on my game,
I kept practicing
until I was.

Soon, I grew to be
as big as my dad.

Now, I was playing in college and winning many games. I soon moved to joining the big guys. My dad was so proud!

It still wasn't easy.
I hurt my foot and couldn't play for a while.

People thought it was the end for me.

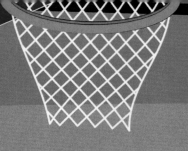

But I pulled through.
Even with my foot hurt,
I never gave up.

Then, I returned, and I showed them why you should keep going.

I became an MVP, and now I'm an all-star.

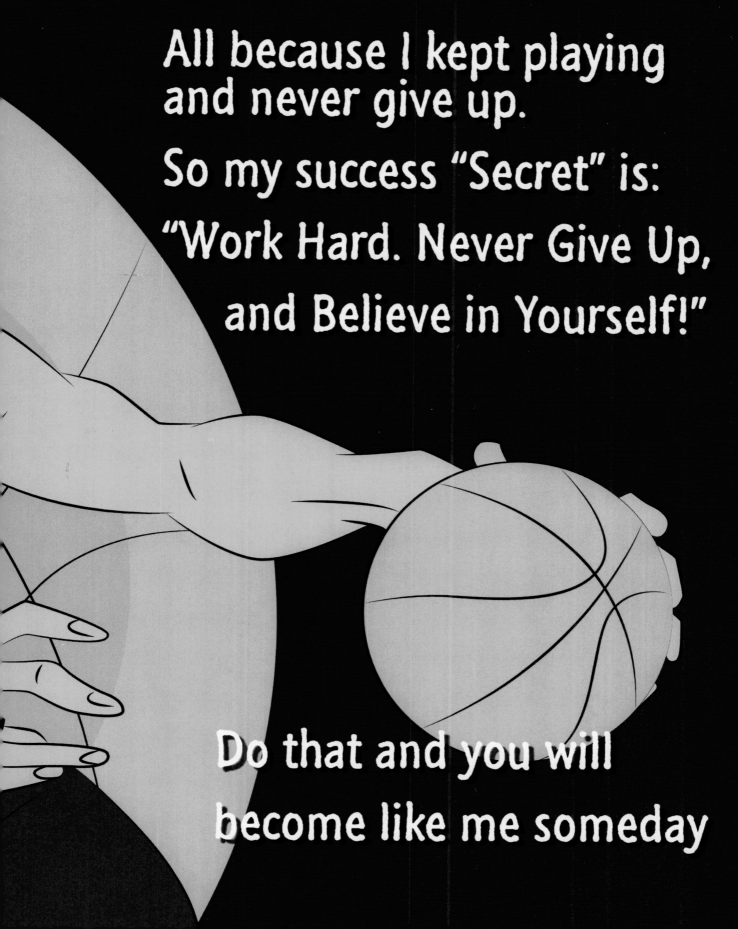

Made in the USA
Lexington, KY
29 November 2018